JULIA MORGAN
Built a
Castle

by CELESTE DAVIDSON MANNIS

illustrated by

MILES HYMAN

Viking

Julia Morgan loved to build.

Born in 1872, Julia was raised in the small California town of Oakland, on San Francisco Bay. Little Julia preferred jumping on the trampoline in her family's barn and chasing her brothers to playing with dolls and having tea parties.

As she grew older, lessons and chores filled Julia's week. But weekends were made for adventure. The Morgans ferried across the bay to San Francisco, where shiny new cable cars climbed the hills, and buildings sprang up like weeds. Julia's father was an engineer who knew how all sorts of things should be built. He enjoyed taking the family on tours through construction sites.

Buildings were huge puzzles. Julia wanted to know how everything fit together.

Sometimes the Morgans traveled across the country, not just across the bay. When they did, Julia visited her cousin Pierre LeBrun, a busy New York architect who designed and directed the building of graceful stone churches, sturdy brick firehouses, and one of the very first skyscrapers in Manhattan—the Metropolitan Life Insurance Tower. Cousin Pierre had the most exciting job in the world!

Julia dreamed of becoming an architect. Architecture combined the study of engineering with special training in the art of building design. But only a few far-away schools taught architecture in those days. So Julia entered the nearby University of California at Berkeley in 1890. There she studied engineering—the only woman in her class—and learned all about how buildings were constructed, and why. There were so many parts to the puzzle:

How do earthquakes, wind, and gravity twist, push, and pull at a building? How is a building anchored to the ground so it doesn't topple? How do columns and beams carry the weight of walls and roofs? When should concrete or steel, wood or brick be used?

Bernard Maybeck, Julia's favorite teacher, helped her put the pieces together. He taught math, but he was an architect, too. Just like Cousin Pierre, he believed that buildings should be as beautifully designed as they were practical and strong. Both men had studied at the greatest school of architecture in the world: the École des Beaux-Arts* in Paris, France.

*École des Beaux-Arts (eh-KOHL deh BOWZ AR) means School of Fine Arts.

After she graduated in 1895, Julia went to work for Maybeck. She studied his designs for everything from rustic hillside cottages to grand university lecture halls.

Maybeck's buildings were planned for the way people would live and work and move within them. But they were also made to inspire, like a magnificent painting or a stirring piece of music.

Julia longed to attend the École des Beaux-Arts and learn more. But that would not be possible. The school only accepted men.

Several months later, a rumor swept through Maybeck's studio. "The École! Have you heard? They may soon open their doors to women!"

Soon wasn't soon enough for Julia Morgan. She packed her trunk and raced cross-country by train. From New York, she boarded a steamship to France.

Paris filled Julia with wonder. She marveled at the Roman ruins of Lutèce, the grinning gargoyles and flying buttresses of Notre Dame, and Gustave Eiffel's infamous iron tower. She saw beauty in the pattern of rooftops and church spires on the horizon, and the glint of gold atop a pyramid she spied from the gardens of the Tuilleries.

Everywhere Julia went, she drew: sometimes in a sketchbook, sometimes on the back of an envelope or even a scrap of paper. Soon Paris felt like an old friend.

The École des Beaux-Arts, however, was not friendly. "A woman study architecture? But why?" The trustees of the École would not even let Julia take their entrance exam. She studied for it anyway, at the *ateliers*, or studios, of two architects who also taught at the École: first Marcel de Monclos, and later, Benjamin Chaussemiche. All the while, she practiced speaking and writing in French.

On weekends, Julia visited museums and rambled through lovely small towns and villages. She explored King Louis XIV's Palace of Versailles, ornate Baroque theaters from the 1600s, and soaring Gothic cathedrals over eight hundred years old. And as she explored, she could almost feel the ghosts of French kings and their royal architects whispering to her.

Every building told a story.

Weeks turned into months and months into a year. Julia moved from a hotel for women to a less expensive apartment on the Rue Guénégaud. Many times she skipped meals to pay for books on architecture.

Suddenly, in the autumn of 1897, the large iron gates of the École creaked open just a bit for Mademoiselle Julia Morgan of California. After a year and a half in Paris, she was allowed to take the school's long and difficult entrance exam. The École made Julia take the exam, not once, not twice, but three times, before she was finally accepted into their architecture program in October of 1898. She was twenty-six years old.

At the École, Monsieur Mazou showed three-dimensional pictures with his stereopticon as he spoke about the history of architecture. Monsieur Monduit described how buildings were constructed from the inside out, down to every last detail. There were countless math courses, countless drawing courses. Julia could hardly wait to start designing buildings. When she did, she remembered all the beautiful buildings she had explored and studied.

Julia won a first-place medal for her final project: an opulent palace theater decorated with statues of characters from Greek mythology. The prize was announced just after her thirtieth birthday, in the spring of 1902.

That year, Julia became the first woman in the history of the École des Beaux-Arts to receive a certificate in architecture.

After six years in France, Julia came home. In 1904, she opened an atelier in San Francisco as California's first licensed woman architect. A flurry of requests to design homes, many for school friends, was followed by a commission from Mills College in Julia's hometown of Oakland. Julia designed a lofty bell tower for the campus, using steel-reinforced concrete to make it strong and more resistant to fire. But some doubted Julia's methods. "It's too expensive! The walls are too thick! What does a woman know about building, anyway?"

In April of 1906 an enormous earthquake and fire ripped through the San Francisco Bay area. Thousands died. San Francisco was all but reduced to rubble and ash. Julia's office was destroyed. But her bell tower stood! As did every other building she had designed. Julia didn't give it much thought. There was a city to rebuild.

Now everybody knew about Julia Morgan. She had completed over 450 projects by the time William Randolph Hearst walked into her office one afternoon in 1919. A very rich, very powerful newspaper publisher, Hearst had grown up in San Francisco, just across the bay from Julia. Though he now lived in New York, every summer he came back to central California to camp on some land he owned in the Santa Lucia Mountains, just above the village of San Simeon. "Miss Morgan," said Mr. Hearst, "we are tired of camping out in the open at the ranch in San Simeon and I would like to build a little something."

What kind of home would suit Mr. Hearst perfectly?

Julia imagined a dramatic showplace where he could entertain both movie stars and presidents and display his huge collection of antique treasures. Ideas blossomed into rough sketches, then careful drawings and watercolor renderings. Mr. Hearst was delighted. Julia prepared plans, details, and models for a large main house to crown the highest hill, and three smaller guesthouses to hug its side. She also designed lush gardens and walkways to connect the buildings and give the project the look and feel of a dreamy hilltop village.

But there was much to do before construction could begin. The road up the hill was a cattle track, and railroads were too far away to deliver supplies. A new road was built, and Mr. Hearst's dock at San Simeon enlarged, so materials could be sent in by ship. Soon, trucks and horsedrawn wagons hauled lumber, iron bars, and tons of cement up the untamed hillside. Bulldozers, cranes, and rock crushers quickly followed.

Workers swarmed to San Simeon: strong men to provide heavy labor and artisans such as carpenters, plasterers, stone-casters, and wood-carvers. Tents, then dormitories, were provided for them, cooks hired to feed them.

Still, it was lonely on the hill. Julia Morgan made certain the men had a movie to watch on the weekend.

The top of the hill was leveled with dynamite, while other areas were pounded flat by teams of horses. Foundations were laid to connect the framework of buildings to the ground. Then walls were erected with concrete, poured layer by layer into wooden forms laced with steel rods. Pipes, electrical wiring, door and window frames were set into the walls. Slowly the buildings began to rise against the hillside.

Walls were finished with limestone and cast stone. A teakwood cornice carved with gargoyles decorated the exterior of the main building, La Casa Grande. Mr. Hearst purchased antique ceilings, moldings, and fireplace mantels from Spain. Julia designed tiles and stained-glass windows.

While she worked on Mr. Hearst's castle, Julia Morgan finished hundreds of other projects for other clients. But come Friday night, she caught the coast train south from San Francisco to San Luis Obispo, and then took a taxi the last fifty-six miles to San Simeon. Julia usually arrived just in time for a quick nap before breakfast. She made this exhausting trip over five hundred times.

Weekends were spent walking the site, meeting with contractors and craftsmen, revising plans, and discussing the project with Mr. Hearst. For many years, Julia worked out of a shack propped against the side of La Casa Grande.

Not everything went according to plan. Once Mr. Hearst had a chimney torn down and moved, then torn down again and put back exactly where it was to begin with. Another time, after Julia remarked on the lovely view from the roof of La Casa Grande, Mr. Hearst asked her to add a third story to the house. Right away! Other additions included a glamorous red velvet movie theater, an airstrip, and a zoo. And then there was the Neptune Pool, a lovely Roman-style pool overlooking the sea, which Julia was asked to redesign five times in twelve years.

Julia Morgan certainly understood Mr. Hearst's passion for building—she shared it! But when Julia disagreed with her flamboyant client, she wasn't afraid to say so. Perhaps that's why William Randolph Hearst, one of the most outspoken and influential men in America, trusted Julia Morgan more than just about anyone.

Julia spent more than half of her almost fifty-year career working on Mr. Hearst's dream home in the hills above San Simeon. Construction finally stopped in 1947, twenty-eight years after it began. But the castle Julia Morgan built tells her story to this day.

⊶⊲ Author's Note ⊳⊶

MY UNLIKELY INTRODUCTION to Julia Morgan was through the pages of a fashion magazine, where evening gown-clad models posed in a fairy-tale castle. A footnote identified the castle as San Simeon, the legendary estate of William Randolph Hearst. What's more, it had been designed and constructed by California architect Julia Morgan. "A woman?" I exclaimed, both surprised and intrigued. So began the research for this book.

Letters Julia wrote to friends and family during her student years in Paris revealed a woman as determined as she was gracious, as vibrant of mind as she was modest of manner. But later, Julia Morgan, architect, didn't talk or write much about her own work. Instead, she felt her work should speak for itself. It does just that.

Classical proportions and flourishes reflect Julia's Beaux-Arts training, especially in projects for universities and other major institutions. But a distinctly California influence shines through. Homes, in particular, seem to grow out of the natural landscape, not dominate it. Julia created this "organic" feeling by building along the natural contours of sites, incorporating local woods and river rock into her designs, and adding decorative touches inspired by native plants and animals.

Yet Julia's primary concern was that her buildings meet the needs of those they served. When building for a family, she had the client's children draw pictures of features they wished their home to include. Not surprisingly, many of these homes contain secret hideaways under stairwells, and mystery doors that lead nowhere.

When Julia was hired to design Saint John's Presbyterian Church in Berkeley, her budget lacked enough money to paint walls and plaster ceilings—so she didn't! Instead, Julia turned unpainted redwood walls and an intricate framework of structural beams and trusses into bold design elements. A potential problem became the catalyst for an architectural masterpiece.

A major commission to repair San Francisco's earthquake-damaged Fairmont Hotel in 1906 was followed by an endless stream of commissions for homes big and small, women's organizations, hospitals, churches, commercial buildings, and eventually, even a castle.

Philanthropist Phoebe Apperson Hearst, William Randolph Hearst's mother, was one of Julia's first patrons and dearest friends. Through Hearst's influence, Julia became a key architect for the Young Women's Christian Association. Julia's biggest project for the YWCA was Asilomar, a seaside conference center and summer camp in Pacific Grove, California. Now a state park, this spectacular Arts and Crafts complex is still enjoyed by thousands of visitors each year.

Of all Julia Morgan's projects, from tiny cottages to fairy-tale castles, my personal favorite is Dodge Chapel, at Asilomar. This lovely sanctuary was designed as a place where young women could both find inspiration and learn skills. Windows flood its polished wood interior with sunshine and frame lush forest views. Alcoves and movable partitions provide intimate spaces for study and conversation. And behind the altar, an enormous picture window overlooks windswept dunes and the boundless blue Pacific.

One glorious spring day, as I sat alone in the sanctuary, the warmth, light, and grace of the structure filled my senses. "Build your dreams," the chapel seemed to say. "Anything is possible."

MORE ABOUT SAN SIMEON

◆ Julia Morgan estimated that construction of San Simeon cost $4,717,000 between 1919 and 1942. During that same twenty-three year period, she earned a total of $70,755 for her work on the project.

◆ La Casa Grande is 60,645 square feet (almost 1 ½ acres) with 115 rooms, including 38 bedrooms and 41 bathrooms. The estate is 90,080 square feet overall, and sits on 128 acres of gardens.

◆ Guests at San Simeon included President Calvin Coolidge; British Prime Minister Winston Churchill; playwright George Bernard Shaw; actors Charlie Chaplin, Greta Garbo, and Cary Grant; as well as aviators Charles Lindbergh, Amelia Earhart, and Howard Hughes.

◆ The zoo at San Simeon was once the largest private zoo in the world: Animals such as lions, polar bears, leopards, and giraffes were safely housed in enclosures, but others, like kangaroos, zebras, and yaks, roamed the hillside. Signs posted on the road to the castle warned, "Animals have the right of way!"

◆ The massive 345,000-gallon Neptune Pool is suspended from reinforced concrete beams, and was engineered by Julia Morgan to sway during earthquakes.

◆ Work on San Simeon slowed down dramatically in 1942 but didn't stop until 1947. Mr. Hearst's ambitious plans for the estate were never fully completed.

To my dad, a long-distance dreamer—C.D.M.

For my children—Juliette, Charlotte, and Eliot—M.H.

ACKNOWLEDGMENTS

Special thanks to Jill Davis, extraordinary friend and editor. To Nancy Loe and her wonderful staff at the Julia Morgan Collection, Cal Poly San Luis Obispo, who graciously extended every professional courtesy to me. To California State Park Ranger Roxann Jacobus, for making "Miss Morgan" and Asilomar sparkle. To Robert Inslee AIA, Katie Henderson, and Michael Yee, who provided invaluable insights into the heart and mind of the architect, and reviewed my manuscript. Sincere thanks also to Regina Hayes, Anne Gunton, Janet Pascal, Denise Cronin, and Nancy Brennan, who shepherded this project expertly through myriad twists and turns, and Miles Hyman for bringing it so vividly to life.–C.D.M.

ADDITIONAL RESOURCES

Sara Holmes Boutelle. *Julia Morgan, Architect.* New York: Abbeville Press, 1988.

Cary James. *Julia Morgan: Architect.* American Women of Achievement. New York: Chelsea House Publishers, 1990.

Nancy E. Loe. *Hearst Castle: An Interpretive History of W. R. Hearst's San Simeon Estate.* Santa Barbara: Companion Press, 1994.

Ginger Wadsworth. *Julia Morgan, Architect of Dreams.* Minneapolis: Lerner Communications, 1990.

www.hearstcastle.com The official website of the Hearst San Simeon State Monument®

Viking

Published by Penguin Group

Penguin Young Readers Group, 345 Hudson Street, New York, New York 10014, U.S.A.

Penguin Books Ltd, Registered Offices: 80 Strand, London WC2R 0RL, England

First published in 2006 by Viking, a division of Penguin Young Readers Group

1 3 5 7 9 10 8 6 4 2

Text copyright © Celeste Davidson Mannis , 2006
Illustrations copyright © Miles Hyman, 2006

LIBRARY OF CONGRESS CATALOGING-IN-PUBLICATION DATA
Mannis, Celeste Davidson.
Julia Morgan / Celeste Mannis, Miles Hyman.
p. cm.
ISBN 0-670-05964-1 (hardcover)
[1. Morgan, Julia, 1872-1957–Juvenile literature. 2. Architects–United States–Biography–Juvenile literature]. I. Hyman, Miles. II. Title.
NA737.M68M36 2005   720'.92–dc22   2004017401

Set in Administer Book
Book design by Nancy Brennan
Manufactured in China

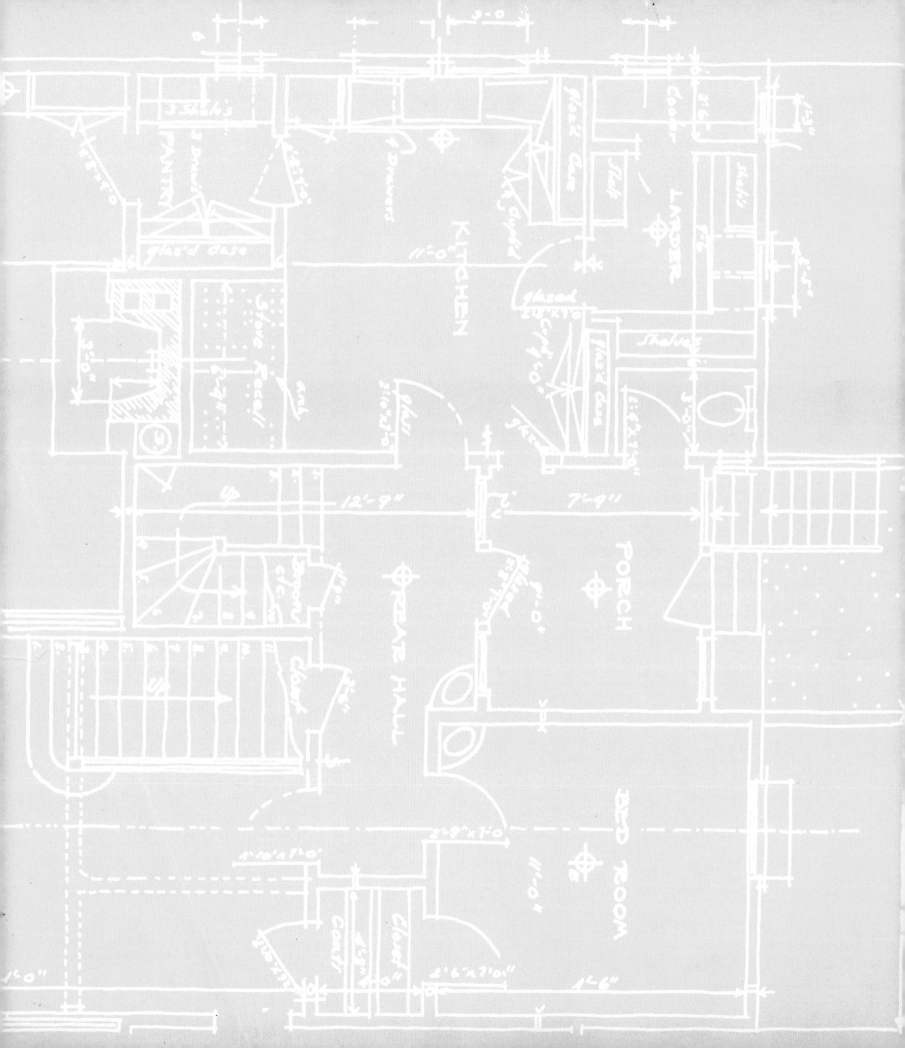